W9-CKB-574

Presented to

_____

by

_____

on

_____

from Susan

With love to my mom, dad, and brother, who taught me that Christmas love and family memories twinkle on long after the last holiday lights have been tucked away.

from Kathy

For Molly and Ryan, our favorite Christmas gifts.

MY GOOD NIGHT Christmas

With Read & Sing-Along CD

by SUSAN L. LINGO
illustrated by KATHY PARKS

Standard Publishing
Cincinnati, Ohio

Standard Publishing, Cincinnati, Ohio
A division of Standex International Corporation

Text © 2001 by Susan L. Lingo
Art © 2001 by Standard Publishing
Sprout logo is a trademark of Standard Publishing
All rights reserved
Printed in Italy

08 07 06 05 04 03 02 01   9 8 7 6 5 4 3 2 1

Project editors: Laura Derico, Lise Caldwell
Art director: Coleen Davis
Graphic arts: Mike Helm, Robert Glover, Jeff Richardson, Bob Korth
Editorial support: Tabitha Neuenschwander, Jennifer Holder
Production director: Linda Ford
Director, Children's Products: Diane Stortz

CD production: Steve Elkins, Wonder Workshop
Narrator: Nan Gurley
Children's vocals: Wonder Kids Choir
Night-Light's voice: Kay DeKalb Smith

Library of Congress Cataloging-in-Publication Data
   Lingo, Susan L.
      My good night Christmas : storybook and CD / written by Susan L. Lingo ; illustrated
  by Kathy Parks.
      p. cm.
   ISBN 0-7847-1205-0
   1. Jesus Christ--Nativity--Juvenile literature. 2. Carols, English--Texts. 3. Preschool
children--Prayer-books and devotions--English. [1. Jesus Christ--Nativity. 2. Christmas.
3. Carols. 4. Bedtime. 5. Prayer books and devotions.] I. Parks, Kathy (Kathleen D.) ill.
II. Title.

BT315.3 .L56 2001
232.92--dc21   00-053338

Scriptures quoted from the *International Children's Bible, New Century Version*, copyright ©1986, 1988
by Word Publishing, Dallas, Texas 75039. Used by permission.

Hello, I'm Night-Light!
Let's read the Christmas story
and listen to the CD together!

A Baby Is Coming!

"He will be great, and people will call him the Son of the Most High." Luke 1:32

God sent his angel Gabriel to tell Mary the most wonderful news.
God was sending the world a Savior—his only Son!
God promised to send his Son to save the world.
God promised to send his Son to love the world.
The angel told Mary that God was pleased with her.
God had chosen Mary to give birth to the special baby.
The angel told Mary to name the baby "Jesus."
Oh, a baby! God's only Son!
A baby to hold. A baby to love.
A baby to save us—sent from heaven above!

Mary thanked God that she was the one he would choose,
then she ran straight to her cousin to tell her the news.
"Elizabeth! Elizabeth! I have news this morn!
God has promised a Savior, and soon he'll be born!
God loves us so much he is sending his Son
to love and forgive us—and my baby's the one!"
Then Elizabeth and Mary gave thanks pure and sweet
for God's perfect promise they knew he would keep.

How many water pots can you count?

O Come, O Come, Emmanuel

O come, O come, Emmanuel,
And ransom captive Israel,
That mourns in lonely exile here
Until the Son of God appear.

Rejoice! Rejoice! Emmanuel
Shall come to thee, O Israel!

O come, Thou Dayspring, come and cheer
Our spirits by Thine advent here;
O drive away the shades of night,
And pierce the clouds and bring us light!

Wow! Wasn't that exciting news that Gabriel brought to Mary? The people needed a Savior and God sent one, just as he had promised! He gave us Jesus, the Light of the world! Mary was so excited as she waited for baby Jesus to be born. When I'm waiting for Christmas, I get excited too! I love to celebrate Jesus' birthday! I light candles at nighttime and thank God for sending his Son to save us and love us.

Dear God, thank you for keeping your promises true, and for sending us Jesus. We love you! Amen.

Close your eyes and think about the good things God promises us. Night-night!

God Keeps His Promises!

Journey to Bethlehem

"So Joseph . . . went to the town of Bethlehem." Luke 2:4

Mary and her husband, Joseph, had to pack. They were going on a trip.
Mary and Joseph were going to the little town of Bethlehem
to be counted with all the other people. Can you count? 1-2-3-4-5.
Mary put blankets on the little donkey.
Joseph put Mary on the little donkey.
Away they went—clip, clip, clop—to Bethlehem.

Clip-clop, clip-clop . . . from evening till morn,
God's special promise was about to be born!
Clip-clop, clip-clop . . . from morning till night,
God was there watching—he kept them in sight!

Soon they came to Bethlehem. Mary was happy.
She knew God's promise was near.
She knew God was watching over them and keeping them safe.
Mary was happy, but she was also very sleepy. Yawwwn!
Even the little donkey yawned. Hee-yawwwn!

Where could they stay? Where could the special baby be born?
Joseph asked the innkeeper if there were any rooms.
"Nope, no room—no room at all.
But try down the street for a stable or stall!"
And though there wasn't a room, Mary wore a smile on her face,
for she knew that God would find them a place!

How many sleepy yawns can you count?

O Little Town of Bethlehem

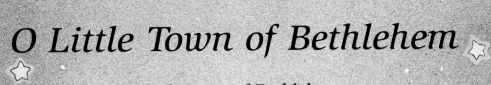

O little town of Bethlehem,
How still we see thee lie!
Above thy deep and dreamless sleep
The silent stars go by.
Yet in thy dark streets shineth
The everlasting Light—
The hopes and fears of all the years
Are met in thee tonight.

O holy Child of Bethlehem,
Descend to us, we pray;
Cast out our sin and enter in—
Be born in us today.
We hear the Christmas angels
The great glad tidings tell;
O come to us, abide with us,
Our Lord Emmanuel!

Yawwwn! Oh my, what a long and sleepy trip it must have been to Bethlehem! I'm glad God was watching out for Mary and Joseph, aren't you? Sometimes at Christmastime, I fly very far to see my family. It's nice to know that God watches over us, at home or away, every night and every day.

Dear God, thank you for keeping us in your sight.
Please keep us safe all through the night. Amen.

Close your eyes and think about how God took care of you today!
Sleep tight!

God Watches Over Us!

Jesus Is Here!

"Today your Savior was born in David's town." Luke 2:11

The night was calm and clear. The city was asleep.
But in a tiny stable in Bethlehem, a miracle unfolded.
In the still of the night, God kept his promise and a baby was born!
Mary gave birth to baby Jesus.
Mary wrapped him in warm, snuggly cloths
and Joseph hugged him with love.
Then Mary laid baby Jesus in a manger.
Mary smiled. Joseph held her hand.
Even the animals knew something wonderful had happened.

The sheep swished their tails, the cows softly mooed.
The kitty cat purred and the doves sweetly cooed.
Baby Jesus just smiled, then closed his eyes
as he nodded to sleep with their soft lullabies.

As baby Jesus slept, Mary thought about how wonderful God is.
God kept his promise and sent his only Son to love and save the world.
What a gift of love!

Mary's heart was filled with the love she was keeping,
for away in a manger the special baby was sleeping.
God sent his Son to love us and free us.
Peace and joy to all! Happy birthday to Jesus!

How many smiling faces do you see?

Away in a Manger

Away in a manger, no crib for a bed,
The little Lord Jesus laid down His sweet head;
The stars in the sky looked down where He lay,
The little Lord Jesus, asleep on the hay.

The cattle are lowing, the Baby awakes,
But little Lord Jesus, no crying He makes;
I love Thee, Lord Jesus! look down from the sky,
And stay by my cradle till morning is nigh.

Be near me, Lord Jesus! I ask Thee to stay
Close by me forever, and love me, I pray;
Bless all the dear children in Thy tender care,
And fit us for heaven, to live with Thee there.

What was *baby Jesus'* first bed? A manger, a feeding box for animals! Filled with hay, it was a nice warm place to sleep. I like to set up the stable scene at Christmastime and put *baby Jesus* in the manger. I look at the little tiny baby and think of God's great big love. Isn't God's love wonderful?

Dear God, thanks for giving the gift of your Son,
and showing your love to everyone. Amen.

As you go to sleep, think about God's great big love for you!
Good night!

God Loves Us!

The Shepherd's Surprise

"I am bringing you some good news. It will be a joy to all the people." Luke 2:10

Sleepy shepherds were watching their fluffy flocks of sheep.
The shepherds had worked hard all day caring for their flocks.
Now they sat still under the quiet, starry sky.
Yawwwn! How sleepy they were!

All of a sudden, a heavenly light glowed like a million stars around them!
Who was there? Who could have such a light?
It was an angel God sent in the night!
The shepherds were very afraid. But the kind angel smiled and said,

"Don't be afraid for I bring you great joy.
A Savior is born—God's own baby boy!
The Lord will love you and bless you and save you from danger.
Go and find the sweet baby asleep in a manger!"

Then more angels—thousands of them!—filled the sky.
The surprised shepherds stared. The surprised shepherds smiled.
And what do you think the shepherds did then?
They hurried to find Jesus!
The shepherds found Jesus as the angel had said,
asleep in a manger instead of a bed.
And when they had seen him, they told everyone
that the Lord had been born and was truly God's Son!
Then the shepherds returned to their flocks on the hill
thanking God for his blessings—and they're praising him still!

How many fluffy sheep do you see?

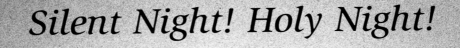

Silent Night! Holy Night!

Silent night! Holy night! All is calm, all is bright
Round yon virgin mother and Child,
Holy Infant, so tender and mild—
Sleep in heavenly peace, Sleep in heavenly peace.

Silent night! Holy night! Shepherds quake at the sight;
Glories stream from heaven afar,
Heavenly hosts sing Alleluia!
Christ the Savior is born! Christ the Savior is born!

Silent night! Holy night! Son of God, love's pure light
Radiant beams from Thy holy face
With the dawn of redeeming grace—
Jesus, Lord, at Thy birth, Jesus, Lord, at Thy birth.

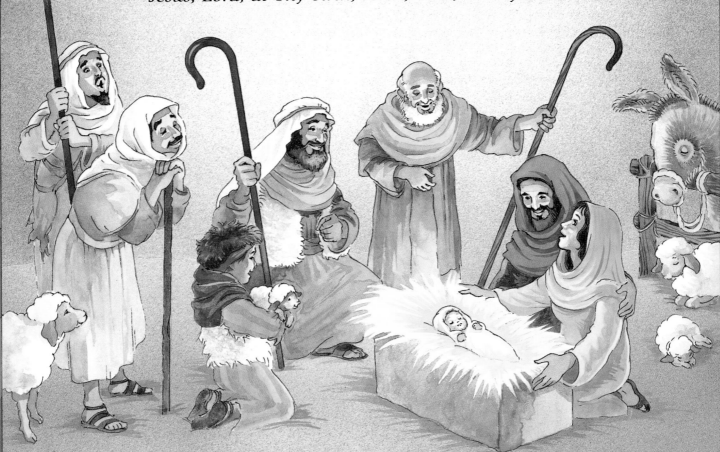

Oh, my! Would you have wanted to be a shepherd? They were so afraid at first. But when they saw Jesus they were filled with joy and oh, so excited! They wanted to tell everyone! I can be like the shepherds now, at Christmas or any time. I can fly here and flit there—I can tell about Jesus everywhere!

Dear God, Thank you for giving us good news and great joy. Help us to tell others about your special boy. Amen.

Think about who you can tell about Jesus and the joy he brings. Night-night!

We Can Tell About Jesus!

Angels All Around

"Give glory to God in heaven, and on earth let there be peace." Luke 2:14

The still night was bright with a heavenly glow.
And the air was joyful with heavenly news!
An angel had just brought the shepherds the good news about Jesus' birth.
Suddenly, many angels were streaming down from heaven above,
praising God with honor and heavenly love!

One, two, three . . .
Too many angels to count or see!
All praising God in the highest;
all filled with angelic glee!
What a heavenly opera,
the loveliest chorus you'd find;
saying, "Glory to God in the highest—
and on earth peace to all of mankind!"

The shepherds were amazed. The sheep hushed their baaaa-ing.
And all the hills near and far, and the moon and the stars
echoed with the angels' lovely voices.
As the angels floated up to heaven,
their last sweet words hung softly in the night air.

The host of heaven sang God's praises;
they sang them again and again,
saying, "Glory to God in the highest—
And on earth peace, goodwill to all men!"

Point to the mouse.

It Came Upon the Midnight Clear

It came upon the midnight clear,
That glorious song of old,
From angels bending near the earth
To touch their harps of gold:
"Peace on the earth, goodwill to men,
From heav'n's all-gracious King!"
The world in solemn stillness lay
To hear the angels sing.

Still thru the cloven skies they come
With peaceful wings unfurled,
And still their heav'nly music floats
O'er all the weary world:
Above its sad and lowly plains
They bend on hov'ring wing,
And ever o'er its Babel sounds
The blessed angels sing.

That glorious song of oooooold! I love to sing Christmas carols, don't you? Singing to God makes me feel happy and good! Oh, singing is a great way to thank God for Jesus, for all his promises, and for his love. The angels sang to thank and praise God and tell everyone how very wonderful he is!

Dear God, we praise you for all that you are and all that you do. We hope our songs tell you how much we love you! Amen.

Think of all the ways we can praise God and tell him we love him. Sleep tight!

We Can Praise God!

They Saw the Star

"When the wise men saw the star, they were filled with joy." Matthew 2:10

Star light, star bright! God hung a star in the Christmas night.
And what a beautiful star it was!
The star was so bright that wise men from the East saw it shining.
They knew something special had happened.
They knew Jesus had been born and they wanted to bring him gifts.

"We'll honor and love him all of our days.
We want to find Jesus to give him our praise!"

So the wise men rode their camels uphill and down,
and followed the star to Bethlehem town.
The shining star stopped over the place where Jesus lay.
The wise men were excited! They would see Jesus that day!

"We'll honor and love him all of our days.
Now we've found Jesus, we'll give him our praise!"

Then the wise men bowed down to worship Jesus.
They opened their treasures and gave Jesus wonderful gifts.
One gift was gold, one smelled very nice,
the other was myrrh and was used as a spice.
What wonderful gifts fit for a king!
And as the wise men left, you might have heard them say,

"We'll honor and love him all of our days—
We want to serve Jesus and give him our praise!"

How many stars can you count?

We Three Kings

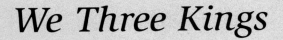

We three kings of Orient are,
Bearing gifts we traverse afar;
Field and fountain, moor and mountain,
Following yonder star.

O star of wonder, star of night,
Star with royal beauty bright,
Westward leading, still proceeding,
Guide us to thy perfect light.

Glorious now behold Him arise,
King and God and Sacrifice;
Alleluia, Alleluia!
Earth to heav'n replies.

Isn't it fun to get presents? It sure is! It's even more fun to give them! Stripes and spots, swirls and dots—I like to wrap up presents at Christmas in all kinds of pretty packages. But most of all, I make sure to wrap my presents with love. God gave a gift to us—his Son—and wrapped it up with lots of love! And we can keep on giving that love to others.

Dear God, help us remember to give to others, and always show love to our sisters and brothers. Amen.

Think of some people you know who could use a gift of love. Good night!

We Can Give God's Love!

Merry Christmas and good night!